Mrs BEETON'S
HOME COOKING

MEAT
DISHES

WARD LOCK LIMITED · LONDON

© Ward Lock Limited 1986

First published in Great Britain
in 1986 by Ward Lock Limited,
8 Clifford Street,
London W1X 1RB,
an Egmont Company.

Edited by Susan Dixon
Designed by Melissa Orrom
Text filmset in Caslon 540
by Cheney & Sons Limited
Printed and bound in Italy
by L.E.G.O.

**British Library Cataloguing in
Publication Data**

Meat.—
(Mrs. Beeton's home cooking)
  1. Cookery (Meat)
  I. Series
  641.6'6   TX749

  ISBN 0-7063-6455-4

Notes
The recipes in this book have
been tested in metric weights
and measures. These have
been based on equivalents of
25g to 1 oz, 500g to 1 lb and
500ml to 1 pint, with some
adjustments where necessary.

It is important to follow *either*
the metric *or* the imperial
measures. Do not use a
combination of measures.

MEAT

HOW TO BUY MEAT ECONOMICALLY.—If the housekeeper is not very particular as to the precise joints to cook for dinner, there is oftentimes an opportunity for her to save as much money in her purchases of meat as will pay for the bread to eat with it. It often occurs, for instance that the butcher may have a superfluity of certain joints, and these he would be glad to get rid of at a reduction of sometimes as much as 1*d.* or 1½*d*, per lb., and thus, in a joint of 8 or 9 lbs., will be saved enough to buy 2 quartern loaves. It frequently happens with many butchers, that, in consequence of a demand for legs and loins of mutton, they have only shoulders left, and these they will be glad to sell at a reduction.

Isabella Beeton 1861

On pages 2 and 3
From the left
Mrs Beeton's Oxford Sausages (page 57), Carbonnade of Beef (page 13) and
Fricassée of Lamb (page 28)

BEEF

Steak Diane

4 helpings

---

4 minute, fillet *or* rump steaks
1 small onion
75g/3oz unsalted butter
grated rind and juice of 1 lemon
1 × 5ml spoon/1 teaspoon caster
  sugar

Worcestershire sauce
1 × 15ml spoon/1 tablespoon
  chopped parsley
2 × 15ml spoons/2 tablespoons
  brandy

In the kitchen, wipe the steaks and trim off any excess fat. Beat them flat with a cutlet bat or rolling-pin until they are no more than 6mm/¼inch thick. Skin the onion and chop it finely. Take all the ingredients to the table.

At the table, melt 50g/2oz of the butter in a large, heavy-based frying pan and fry the onion for about 5 minutes until soft. Remove the onion from the pan and keep warm on a plate. Raise the heat under the pan. Using the remaining butter, fry 2 steaks at a time over high heat for 1 minute on each side. Remove from the pan and keep warm. Return the onions to the pan, and add the lemon rind and juice, the sugar, and a few drops of Worcestershire sauce. Stir in the parsley and cook lightly. Warm the brandy. Put the steaks into the pan and flame with the warmed brandy. Serve immediately, with the sauce spooned over them, and with chipped potatoes, grilled mushrooms and/or tomatoes.

Steak Diane

STEAKS WITH MUSTARD SAUCE

4 helpings

4 fillet *or* sirloin steaks
freshly ground pepper
25g/1oz unsalted butter
2×15ml spoons/2 tablespoons oil
150ml/6fl oz soured cream

1×5ml spoon/1 teaspoon lemon
    juice
2×5ml spoons/2 teaspoons French
    mustard
salt

Wipe the steaks and trim off any excess fat. Beat each steak lightly on both sides with a cutlet bat or rolling pin. Season with pepper. Heat the butter and oil in a heavy-based frying pan. When hot, put in the steaks and fry quickly on both sides for 6–8 minutes according to requirement. Lift out the steaks, transfer them to a warmed serving dish, and keep hot. Stir the soured cream into the juices in the pan and cook gently, without boiling. Stir in the lemon juice, mustard, and salt to taste. Pour the mustard sauce over the steaks and serve at once.

HOT BEEF PIE

6 helpings

750g/1½lb stewing steak
    (chuck, blade *or* neck)
3 medium-sized onions
3 large carrots

1kg/2lb potatoes
salt and pepper
beef stock *or* water as required

Wipe the meat and trim of any excess fat. Cut the meat into 2.5cm/1 inch cubes. Prepare the vegetables. Slice the onions and carrots thinly, and cut the potatoes into slices about 6mm/¼ inch thick. Arrange the meat, onion, carrot, and potato slices in layers in a 2 litre/4 pint casserole, finishing with a neat layer of potatoes. Season with salt and pepper. Three-quarters cover the meat and vegetables with stock or water (add more during cooking if the dish seems dry). Cover the pan with a tight-fitting lid and cook in a warm oven, 160°C/325°F/Gas 3, for 2 hours.

Uncover 30 minutes before the end of the cooking time to allow the top layer of potato to brown. Serve from the casserole.

POTATOES.

MRS BEETON'S ROAST RIBS OF BEEF

6–8 helpings

2.5kg/5lb forerib of beef
flour for dredging

50–75g/2–3oz clarified dripping
   (see **Note**)
salt and pepper

GARNISH

shredded horseradish

Ask the butcher to trim the thin ends of the rib bones so that the joint will stand upright. Wipe the meat but do not salt it. Dredge it lightly with flour. Melt 50g/2oz dripping in a roasting tin and brush some of it over the meat. Put the meat in the tin and roast it in a very hot oven, 230°C/450°F/Gas 8, for 10 minutes. Baste well, reduce heat to moderate, 180°C/350°F/Gas 4, and continue to roast for 1¾ hours for rare meat, or 2¼ hours for well-done meat. Baste frequently during cooking, using extra dripping if required.

When cooked, salt the meat lightly. Transfer the joint to a warmed serving dish and keep hot. Pour off almost all the fat in the roasting tin, leaving the sediment. Pour in enough water to make a thin gravy, then heat to boiling point, stirring all the time. Taste, and season with salt and pepper. Strain the gravy into a warmed gravy-boat. Garnish the dish with 1 or 2 small heaps of shredded horseradish.

Note To clarify dripping, put the dripping into a large saucepan and add about the same volume of cold water. Heat very gently until the water begins to boil, removing the scum as it rises. Allow to simmer for about 5 minutes, then strain into a bowl and leave to cool and solidify. Remove the fat in one piece, dry it on soft kitchen paper and scrape away the sediment from underneath. Heat the fat very slowly until all bubbling ceases, to drive off any water.

Mrs Beeton's Roast Ribs of Beef

BEEF À LA MODE

1kg/2lb rump of beef
25g/1oz butter *or* dripping
10 button onions
25g/1oz plain flour
750ml/1½ pints beef stock

salt and pepper
2 rashers streaky bacon, without
  rinds
2 medium-sized carrots

MARINADE

1 small onion
100ml/4fl oz claret
juice of ½ lemon

2 cloves
salt and pepper
bouquet garni

Wipe, trim, and tie the meat into a neat shape if necessary.

Make the marinade first. Skin and chop the onion finely. Mix all the ingredients for the marinade, put in the meat, and leave to stand for 2 hours, basting frequently. Drain the beef thoroughly, and strain and reserve the marinade.

Heat the butter or dripping in a large stewpan and fry the meat in the hot fat, turning it until browned on all sides. Skin the button onions and fry at the same time, turning them so that they brown evenly. Remove the beef and onions and put to one side. Stir the flour into the fat in the pan and cook until browned. Gradually add the stock and the marinade and stir until boiling. Replace the meat and onions. Season to taste. Cover the top of the meat with the bacon. Slice the carrots thinly, then add them to the pan. Cover with a tight-fitting lid and cook gently for 2½ hours, stirring occasionally, or transfer to an ovenproof dish, cover, and cook in a warm oven, 160°C/325°F/Gas 3, for 2 hours. When tender, transfer the meat to a warmed serving dish and keep hot. Strain the liquid in the stewpan or casserole, and pour it over the meat.

Note If liked, the bacon, onions, and carrots can be served with the meat although they will have given up most of their food value during the long, slow cooking.

CARBONNADE OF BEEF

— 6 helpings —

750g/1½lb stewing steak (chuck, blade, skirt *or* thin flank)
50g/2oz dripping
2 large onions
1 clove of garlic
1×15ml spoon/1 tablespoon plain flour
250ml/½ pint beef stock *or* water
375ml/¾ pint brown ale
salt and pepper
bouquet garni
a pinch of grated nutmeg
a pinch of light soft brown sugar
1×5ml spoon/1 teaspoon red wine vinegar
6 thin slices from a French bâton loaf
1×15ml spoon/1 tablespoon French mustard *or* 1×15ml spoon/1 tablespoon English mustard mixed with vinegar to taste

Wipe the meat and trim off any excess fat. Cut the meat into 2.5–3.75cm/1–1½ inch cubes. Heat the dripping in a large pan. Fry the meat quickly until brown on all sides. Transfer to a casserole and keep warm. Skin and slice the onions and fry them in the fat in the pan until lightly browned. Skin and crush the garlic, add it to the onions and fry gently for 1 minute. Pour off any excess fat. Sprinkle the flour over the onion and garlic and cook, stirring until just beginnning to brown. Gradually stir in the stock or water, and the ale. Add the salt and pepper, bouquet garni, nutmeg, sugar, and vinegar. Heat to boiling point and pour the liquid over the meat in the casserole. Cover, and cook in a warm oven, 160°C/325°F/Gas 3, for 1½–2 hours.

When cooked, remove the bouquet garni, spread the slices of bread with mustard, and press them well down into the gravy. Return the casserole, uncovered, to the oven, for about 15 minutes to allow the bread to brown slightly. Serve from the casserole.

IRISH SPICED BEEF

(for Christmas)

3kg/6lb lean boned joint of beef
1×5ml spoon/1 teaspoon ground
   allspice
1×5ml spoon/1 teaspoon ground
   cloves

3 carrots
3 medium-sized onions
a bundle of fresh mixed herbs *or*
   bouquet garni
250ml/½ pint stout

SPICING MIXTURE

1×5ml spoon/1 teaspoon ground
   cloves
6 blades mace
1×5ml spoon/1 teaspoon
   peppercorns
1×5ml spoon/1 teaspoon allspice

3×15ml spoons/3 tablespoons soft
   light brown sugar
2×5ml spoons/2 teaspoons
   saltpetre
500g/1lb coarse salt
3 bay leaves
1 clove of garlic

Make the spicing mixture first. Mix all the dry ingredients together, then pound in the bay leaves and garlic. Stand the meat in a large earthenware or glass dish, and rub the spicing mixture thoroughly all over it. Repeat every day for a week, taking the spicing mixture from the bottom of the dish. Turn the meat over twice. At the end of the week, wash the meat and tie it into a convenient shape for cooking.

Sprinkle the allspice and cloves over the meat. Prepare and chop the carrots and the onions. Make a bed of the vegetables and the herbs in a large saucepan. Put the meat on top. Barely cover with warm water, cover with a lid, and simmer gently for 5 hours. Add the stout for the last hour of the cooking time.

Serve hot or cold (At Christmas, the beef is usually served cold, in slices). To serve cold, remove the hot meat from the cooking liquid, and press between 2 dishes, with a weight on top, until cold.

Irish Spiced Beef

MRS BEETON'S BOILED MARROW BONES

2 pieces of marrow bone per helping

marrow bones
  (150g/5oz each)

flour

Choose marrow bones from the leg or shin. Ask your butcher to saw them across into pieces 7.5cm/3 inches long, or do it yourself. Shape the thick ends by chopping them so that the bones will stand upright. Mix some flour to a stiff paste with water, and plaster this paste over the open end of each bone to seal in the marrow. Tie each bone in a floured cloth.

Stand the bones upright in a deep saucepan containing enough boiling water to come half-way up the bones. Cover the pan with a tight-fitting lid, reduce the heat, and simmer gently for about 1½ hours. Refill the pan with boiling water, if necessary. When cooked, remove the bones from the cloth and scrape off the paste. Fasten a paper napkin round each one and serve with a pointed teaspoon to extract the marrow.

Serve with Melba or hot dry toast and a seasoning of pepper.

SHEPHERD'S PIE

4–6 helpings

625g/1¼lb lean beef mince
2 medium-sized onions
25g/1oz dripping
1×15ml spoon/1 tablespoon flour
150ml/6fl oz strong beef stock
salt and freshly ground black
  pepper

750g/1½lb potatoes
a pinch of grated nutmeg
milk
1–2×15ml spoons/1–2 tablespoons
  butter (optional)
butter for greasing

Break up any lumps in the meat with a fork. Skin and slice the onions. Melt the dripping in a saucepan, and fry the onions until softened but not coloured. Stir in the flour, and cook gently for 1–2 minutes, stirring all the time. Gradually add the stock, without letting lumps form, and stir until boiling. Reduce the heat, and simmer for 2–3 minutes until the sauce thickens. Stir in the mince, cover the pan, and simmer for 20 minutes. Season well, replace the lid, and simmer for 10 minutes longer or until the mince is cooked through and tender.

Meanwhile, prepare the potatoes and boil them in salted water until tender. Mash them until smooth with a seasoning of salt, pepper and nutmeg, enough milk to make them creamy, and butter, if liked. Put the meat and sauce into a greased pie dish or shallow oven-to-table baking dish. Cover with the potato, smooth the top, then flick it up into small peaks or score a pattern on the surface with a fork. Bake for 10–15 minutes in a hot oven, 220°C/425°F/Gas 7, until browned on top. Serve hot.

Overleaf
From the back, clockwise
Hot Beef Pie (page 9), *Shepherd's Pie (above)* and
Exeter Stew (page 21)

MEATBALLS IN SPICY SAUCE

4 helpings

1 small onion
1 small clove of garlic
400g/13oz raw minced beef
50g/2oz soft white breadcrumbs
2×15ml spoons/2 tablespoons
   chopped parsley

salt and pepper
2 eggs
3×15ml spoons/3 tablespoons
   cooking *or* olive oil

SPICY SAUCE

2×15ml spoons/2 tablespoons oil
2 small onions
1 stick of celery
2×15ml spoons/2 tablespoons
   concentrated tomato purée
1×15ml spoon/1 tablespoon
   Worcestershire sauce

Tabasco sauce
1×15ml spoon/1 tablespoon
   vinegar
1×5ml spoon/1 teaspoon made
   mustard
300ml/12fl oz water
salt and pepper

Make the sauce first. Heat the oil in a saucepan. Skin and chop the onions. Wash and chop the celery finely. Fry the onions and celery gently in the oil until softened. Add the tomato purée, and mix well. Stir in the Worcestershire and Tabasco sauces, the vinegar, mustard, and water. Season with salt and pepper. Heat to boiling point, reduce the heat, cover with a lid, and simmer for about 25 minutes.

Prepare the meatballs. Skin and chop the onion finely and skin and crush the garlic. Mix together the onion, garlic, meat, breadcrumbs, parsley, and seasoning. Beat the eggs until liquid and use to bind the meat mixture. Divide into sixteen pieces and shape into balls. Heat the oil in a frying pan. Add the meatballs and fry, turning frequently, until browned all over. Drain the excess oil and fat from the pan. Pour in the spicy sauce, cover the pan with a tight-fitting lid, and cook for about 45 minutes.

EXETER STEW

750g/1½lb chuck steak *or* blade *or* neck of beef
3×10ml spoons/3 dessertspoons dripping
3 medium-sized onions

3×15ml spoons/3 tablespoons plain flour
625ml/1¼ pints water
1×5ml spoon/1 teaspoon vinegar
salt and pepper

SAVOURY PARSLEY BALLS

100g/4oz plain flour
½×2.5ml spoon/¼ teaspoon baking powder
4½×15ml spoons/4½ tablespoons shredded suet
1×15ml spoon/1 tablespoon finely chopped parsley

1×2.5ml spoon/½ teaspoon dried mixed herbs
1×5ml spoon/1 teaspoon salt
1×2.5ml spoon/½ teaspoon ground pepper
1 egg *or* 3×15ml spoons/3 tablespoons milk

Wipe the meat and trim off any excess fat. Cut the meat into 5cm/2 inch cubes. Heat the dripping in a stewpan and fry the meat and put to one side. Skin and slice the onions. Put them in the pan, and fry gently until light brown. Add the flour and cook, stirring until browned. Mix in the water and stir until boiling. Reduce the heat to simmering point. Add the vinegar and seasoning to taste. Return the meat, cover the pan, and simmer gently for 1½ hours.

To make the parsley balls, sift the flour and baking powder into a bowl. Add the suet, herbs, salt and pepper, and mix together. Beat the egg, if used, until liquid and bind the dry ingredients together with the beaten egg or milk to form a stiff dough. Divide the dough into 12 equal pieces and roll each into a ball.

Heat the stew to boiling point and drop in the balls. Reduce the heat and simmer for a further 30 minutes with the pan half-covered. Pile the meat in the centre of a warmed serving dish, pour the gravy over it and arrange the balls neatly round the base.

LAMB

ROAST LEG OF LAMB

a leg of lamb *or* mutton   oil *or* fat for basting
salt and pepper

Weigh the leg joint to calculate the cooking time, allowing 20 minutes per 500g/1lb plus 20 minutes extra. Wipe the meat. Place the leg on a wire rack, if available, in a shallow roasting tin. Season the meat, and either pour over it a little oil or rub it with a little fat. Place the roasting tin in the oven, and cook in a very hot oven 230°C/450°F/Gas 8, for about 10 minutes to sear or brown the outside of the meat and seal in the juices. Reduce the temperature to fairly hot, 190°C/375°F/Gas 5, to finish the cooking.

Transfer the cooked meat from the oven to a warmed meat dish, and keep hot. Prepare a gravy, if liked, from the sediment in the roasting tin.

Serve with mint sauce.

Roast Leg of Lamb

BAKED LAMB OR MUTTON CUTLETS WITH MUSHROOMS

6 helpings

6 cutlets from best end of neck of
   lamb *or* mutton
salt and pepper

fat for greasing
200g/7oz button mushrooms
1 × 10ml spoon/1 dessertspoon oil
   or butter

Wipe and trim the cutlets neatly. Season the cutlets on both sides
and place them in a single layer in a greased casserole or ovenproof
dish. Clean the mushrooms and scatter them over the cutlets.
Season to taste with salt and pepper, and sprinkle with oil or dot
with pats of butter. Cover with a tight-fitting lid and bake in a cool
oven, 150°C/300°F/Gas 2, for 1–1½ hours, until the cutlets are
tender.

LAMB OR MUTTON SHASHLIK

4 helpings

500g/1lb boned leg of lamb *or* mutton
50g/2oz butter
200g/7oz lean bacon

8 button onions
8 bay leaves
salt and pepper

Wipe the meat and trim off any excess fat. Cut the meat into 2.5cm/1 inch cubes. Heat 25g/1oz of the butter in a pan and brown the meat on all sides. Cut the bacon into slightly smaller cubes. Skin the onions and parboil them in slightly salted water for 3 minutes. Drain. Divide the meat, bacon, onions, and bay leaves into four portions and thread each portion on to a long skewer. Season with salt and pepper. Melt the remaining butter and brush it over the meat, bacon, and onions on the skewers. Grill under high heat, or over a charcoal fire, turning the skewers occasionally, for 8–10 minutes until the meat is well browned.

Serve with boiled rice.

MUTTON CUTLETS.

LAMB CUTLETS IN ASPIC

8 helpings

8 cutlets from best end of leg of
   lamb
salt and pepper

750ml/1½ pints aspic jelly

GARNISH

100g/4oz cooked green peas
100g/4oz cooked sliced green
   beans

2×15ml spoons/2 tablespoons
   mayonnaise *or* French dressing
½ lettuce

Wipe and trim the cutlets neatly. Season with salt and pepper. Either grill, shallow fry or braise the cutlets. Although grilling and frying are simpler and quicker methods, braising is recommended because it imparts extra flavour. When cooked, leave the cutlets until cold, covered with a light cloth.

Melt the aspic jelly and pour a thin layer of it into a large dish rinsed with cold water. Leave to set. Cool the remaining jelly until cold but not set. Brush the cutlets with the cold, liquid aspic and lay them about 1.25cm/½ inch apart on the jelly, with each bone curving the same way. Pour the remaining jelly gently over the cutlets and leave to set. Then turn out on to a sheet of greaseproof paper laid on a chilled metal tray.

Mix the cooked peas and beans with the mayonnaise or French dressing and spoon them into the centre of a round dish. With a sharp knife dipped in hot water, cut out the cutlets and arrange them in a circle around the dish, with the bones pointing inwards. Shred the lettuce and arrange it outside the circle of cutlets. Chop the aspic remaining in the dish and use to garnish the cutlets.

Lamb Cutlets in Aspic

FRICASSÉE OF LAMB

4–6 helpings

a breast of lamb
   (750g/1½lb approx)
1 medium-sized onion
50g/2oz dripping *or* lard *or*
   margarine
2 bay leaves
2 cloves

1 blade of mace
6 white peppercorns
salt and pepper
500ml/1 pint water
25g/1oz plain flour
500g/1lb creamed potatoes

GARNISH

1×10ml spoon/1 dessertspoon
   roughly chopped capers

Wipe the meat, bone it, if not already done by the butcher, and trim of any excess fat. Cut the meat into 5cm/2 inch squares. Skin and slice the onion. Melt the fat in a stewpan, add the meat, onion, bay leaves, cloves, mace, peppercorns, and salt and pepper to taste. Half cover the pan and cook very gently for about 30 minutes, stirring often. Meanwhile, heat the water to boiling point. Add it to the pan, and simmer, covered, for about 1½ hours or until the meat is tender.

Blend the flour to a smooth paste with a small quantity of cold water in a saucepan. Strain the liquid from the meat, measure off 250ml/½ pint liquid, and gradually stir it into the blended flour. Bring to the boil, stirring all the time, and boil for 2–3 minutes. Add this sauce to the meat and re-heat if necessary. Spoon or pipe the hot creamed potatoes in a border on a warmed serving dish and arrange the meat in the centre. Sprinkle the chopped capers over the meat.

HARICOT OF LAMB OR MUTTON

---
6 helpings

1kg/2lb middle neck of lamb *or*
    scrag end of mutton
25g/1oz butter *or* dripping
1 large onion
2 cloves garlic

25g/1oz plain flour
800ml/1 pint 12fl oz chicken stock
bouquet garni
salt and pepper

GARNISH

2 carrots   1 turnip

Wipe the meat and trim off any skin and excess fat. Cut the meat into serving-sized pieces or cutlets. Melt the fat in a large saucepan and fry the meat quickly until sealed and lightly browned. Skin and chop the onion, and skin and crush the garlic. Fry them in the fat until softened but not coloured. Stir in the flour and cook gently until browned. Draw the pan off the heat and gradually add the stock. Return to the heat and stir until boiling. Add the bouquet garni, seasoning, and meat. Cover with a lid and simmer over gentle heat for about 2 hours until the meat is tender.

Meanwhile, prepare the carrots and turnip for the garnish and cut them into 6mm/¼ inch dice. Add the vegetable trimmings to the meat whilst it is cooking. Cook the diced vegetables separately from the meat in boiling salted water until just tender.

When cooked, arrange the meat on a warmed serving dish. If necessary, boil the stock in the saucepan rapidly to reduce it, then strain it over the meat. Garnish the meat with the cooked diced vegetables.

IRISH STEW

4–6 helpings

1kg/2lb middle neck *or* scrag end of
   neck of lamb *or* mutton
2 large onions

1kg/2lb potatoes
salt and pepper
water as required

GARNISH

2×15ml spoons/2 tablespoons
   chopped parsley

Wipe the meat, cut it into neat cutlets or pieces, and trim off any excess fat. Skin the onions and slice them thinly; prepare and slice the potatoes. In a stewpan, place the layers of meat, onions, and potatoes, adding seasoning between each layer, and finishing with a layer of potatoes. Add enough water to come half-way up the meat and vegetables. Cover the pan with a lid, heat to simmering point, and simmer gently for 2½ hours. Alternatively, cook the stew in a casserole, covered with a lid, in a fairly hot oven, 190°C/375°F/Gas 5, for 2–2½ hours. Serve garnished with chopped parsley.

Irish Stew

BLANQUETTE OF LAMB

5–6 helpings

1kg/2lb lean best end of neck *or* middle neck *or* breast of lamb
salt and pepper
water to cover
1 large onion
bouquet garni
6 black peppercorns
a pinch of grated nutmeg

2×15ml spoons/2 tablespoons butter *or* margarine
2×15ml spoons/2 tablespoons plain flour
1 egg yolk
2×15ml spoons/2 tablespoons single cream *or* milk

GARNISH
100g/4oz baked button mushrooms

Wipe the meat. Bone it and cut into pieces about 5cm/2 inches square. Put the meat into a stewpan with the salt and water to cover. Heat to boiling point. Skin and slice the onion and add it to the pan with the bouquet garni, peppercorns, and nutmeg. Reduce the heat, cover the pan with a tight-fitting lid, and simmer for 1½–2 hours until the meat is tender. When cooked, transfer the meat to a warmed serving dish, cover, and keep hot. Strain the liquid from the meat and measure off 250ml/½ pint.

Melt the butter or margarine in a saucepan, stir in the flour, and cook gently for 2–3 minutes without browning it. Gradually add the stock and stir until boiling, then reduce the heat and simmer for 3 minutes. Beat together the egg yolk and the cream or milk. Stir a little of the hot sauce into the egg yolk mixture, then add the mixture to the rest of the sauce off the heat. Return to the heat, stir, and cook very gently until the egg yolk thickens the sauce, but do not allow the sauce to boil or it may curdle. Season to taste. Strain the sauce over the meat. Garnish with the button mushrooms.

LAMB OR MUTTON ROLL

6 helpings

650g/1lb 5oz lean ham *or* mutton
200g/7oz ham *or* bacon
1×2.5ml spoon/½ teaspoon finely
  chopped onion
3×15ml spoons/3 tablespoons soft
  white breadcrumbs
1×5ml spoon/1 teaspoon chopped
  parsley
½×2.5ml spoon/¼ teaspoon dried
  mixed herbs
a pinch of grated nutmeg

1×2.5ml spoon/½ teaspoon grated
  lemon rind
salt and pepper
1 egg
2×15ml spoons/2 tablespoons
  chicken stock
1×15ml spoon/1 tablespoon plain
  flour *or* beaten egg and 2×15ml
  spoons/2 tablespoons
  breadcrumbs
2×15ml spoons/2 tablespoons
  dripping

Wipe the lamb or mutton. Finely chop or mince all the meat. Put in a bowl and mix it well with the onion, breadcrumbs, herbs, nutmeg, and grated lemon rind. Season to taste. Beat the egg until liquid, and add it with the stock to moisten the mixture. Shape it into a short thick roll. Wrap the roll in foil or several thicknesses of greaseproof paper to keep it in shape and to protect the meat. Bake in a moderate oven, 180°C/350°F/Gas 4, for 1½ hours.

Remove the foil or paper and lightly dredge the roll with the flour, or brush it with the beaten egg and coat it with breadcrumbs. Heat the dripping in a baking tin and place the roll in the tin. Baste well and return it to the oven for a further 30 minutes until browned.

Serve with gravy.

Note Under-cooked cold lamb or mutton can be used. The roll should then be cooked for only 1 hour before browning it.

MOUSSAKA

1 medium-sized aubergine
salt
1 large onion
1 clove of garlic
2 medium-sized tomatoes
2×15ml spoons/2 tablespoons olive
   oil
500g/1lb raw lamb, minced
pepper

1×10ml spoon/1 dessertspoon
   parsley
150ml/6fl oz dry white wine
300ml/12fl oz milk
1 egg
2 egg yolks
a pinch of grated nutmeg
75g/3oz Kefalotiri *or* Parmesan
   cheese
fat for greasing

Cut the aubergine into 1.25cm/½ inch slices, sprinkle them with salt and put to one side on a large platter to drain. Chop the onion, grate the garlic, and skin, de-seed, and chop the tomatoes. Heat the olive oil, add the onion and garlic, and sauté gently until the onion is soft. Add the minced meat, and continue cooking, stirring with a fork to break up any lumps in the meat. When the meat is thoroughly browned, add salt, pepper, parsley, and the tomatoes. Mix well, and add the white wine. Simmer the mixture for a few minutes to blend the flavours, then remove from the heat.

In a basin, beat together the milk, egg, egg yolks, salt, and a good pinch of grated nutmeg. Grate the cheese, add about half to the egg mixture, and beat again briefly.

Grease a 20×10×10cm/8×4×4 inch oven-to-table baking dish. Drain the aubergine slices and pat dry with soft kitchen paper. Place half in the bottom of the casserole and cover with the meat mixture. Lay the remaining aubergine slices on the meat and pour the milk and egg mixture over them. Sprinkle the remaining cheese on top. Bake in a moderate oven, 180°C/350°F/Gas 4, for 30–40 minutes, until the custard is set and the top is light golden-brown. Serve from the dish.

Note Moussaka can be made a day ahead, then re-heated, covered in a warm oven.

Moussaka

DEVILLED KIDNEYS

4 helpings

4 sheep's *or* 8 lamb's kidneys
3 × 10ml spoons/3 dessertspoons dripping *or* oil
1 × 15ml spoon/1 tablespoon chopped onion
1 × 2.5ml spoon/½ teaspoon salt
½ × 2.5ml spoon/¼ teaspoon Cayenne pepper
1 × 15ml spoon/1 tablespoon chutney

2 × 5ml spoons/2 teaspoons lemon juice
1 × 2.5ml spoon/½ teaspoon prepared mustard
125ml/¼ pint beef stock
2 egg yolks
soft white breadcrumbs

Skin, core, and cut the kidneys in half lengthways, then cut them into neat pieces. Heat the dripping or oil in a small pan, add the onion, and cook gently until softened but not browned. Add the kidney, salt, Cayenne pepper, chutney, lemon juice, mustard, and stock. Heat to boiling point, reduce the heat, cover the pan, and simmer gently for 15–20 minutes, until the kidney is cooked. Cool slightly. Beat the egg yolks lightly and stir them in. Sprinkle in enough breadcrumbs to make the mixture a soft consistency. Re-season if required.

Serve on buttered toast or in a border of hot creamed potatoes.

KIDNEYS.

LIVER HOT POT

6 helpings

500g/1lb sheep's *or* lamb's liver
3×15ml spoons/3 tablespoons
   plain flour
salt and pepper
800g/1lb 10oz potatoes
2 large onions

fat for greasing
500ml/1 pint beef stock
6 rashers streaky bacon, without
   rinds

Remove the skin and tubes from the liver. Season the flour with salt and pepper. Dip each slice of liver in the seasoned flour. Prepare the potatoes and onions and slice them thinly. Arrange layers of liver, onion, and potatoes in a greased casserole, ending with a neat layer of potatoes. Heat the stock and pour in just enough to cover the potatoes. Cover the casserole with a lid. Bake in a moderate oven, 180°C/350°F/Gas 4, for about 1 hour or until the liver is tender.

    Remove the lid and arrange the bacon rashers on top. Continue cooking without a lid until the bacon is crisp. Serve from the casserole.

VEAL

STUFFED BREAST OF VEAL

6 helpings

a thick end of breast of veal
   (1kg/2lb approx)
salt and pepper
300g/10oz pork sausage-meat
1 large onion
1 large carrot
½ turnip

bouquet garni
6 black peppercorns
water to cover
butter for greasing
250g/8oz short-grain rice
50g/2oz grated Parmesan cheese

GARNISH

slices of lemon

Remove all bones and tendons from the meat. Wipe, then season well. Spread the sausage-meat evenly over the inner surface of the meat, roll up and tie securely with fine string. Prepare and slice the vegetables. Put them with the bones and trimmings in a large pan. Add the bouquet garni, peppercorns, salt and pepper, and enough water to cover the vegetables. Place the meat on top, cover with buttered greaseproof paper and a tight-fitting lid. Heat to boiling point, reduce the heat and simmer gently for about 2½ hours. Baste occasionally and add more water if necessary. Transfer the meat to a warmed dish and keep hot.

Strain off the liquid and make it up to 750ml/1½ pints with water. Put the stock in a pan and bring to the boil. Wash the rice and cook it in the stock until the stock is absorbed. Season to taste and stir in the cheese. Place the rice in a layer on a warmed serving dish and put the meat on top. Garnish with slices of lemon.

Suffed Breast of Veal

ESCALOPES OF VEAL

(Wiener Schnitzel)

6 thin escalopes of veal
   (12.5×7.5cm/5×3 inches
   approx)
plain flour
salt and pepper
1 egg

2–3 drops oil
dried white breadcrumbs for
  coating
butter *or* oil and butter for frying

GARNISH

6 crimped lemon slices

1×15ml spoon/1 tablespoon
  chopped parsley

Wipe the meat. Season the flour with salt and pepper. Dip the escalopes in the seasoned flour. Beat the egg until liquid with the oil. Brush the escalopes with the egg mixture and coat with breadcrumbs, pressing them on well. Heat the butter or mixture of oil and butter in a large frying pan. Put in the escalopes and fry over moderate to gentle heat for 7–10 minutes, turning them once only.

Remove the escalopes and place them, overlapping slightly, on a warmed, flat serving dish. Garnish the middle of each escalope with a crimped slice of lemon sprinkled with parsley.

BARDED ROAST BEST END NECK OF VEAL

a best end of neck of veal (1kg/2lb approx)
larding bacon
2 medium-sized carrots
1 medium-sized onion
1 small turnip
2 sticks celery
salt
bouquet garni
10 white peppercorns
125–250ml/¼–½ pint chicken stock
butter for greasing
fat *or* oil for basting
25g/1oz butter *or* margarine
25g/1oz plain flour

Wipe the meat. Fold the flap of meat under the joint. Bard the upper surface (flesh side) in close rows with thin 3.75cm/1½ inch strips of fat bacon. Prepare and slice the carrots, onion, turnip and celery. Put the vegetables in a large pan with the salt, bouquet garni, peppercorns, and just enough stock to cover them. Lay the meat on top, cover with buttered greaseproof paper and a tight-fitting lid, and cook gently for 2 hours. Add more stock, if needed.

When cooked, remove the meat from the pan. Heat some fat or oil in a roasting tin. Put the meat into the hot fat or oil, baste well and bake in a moderate oven, 180°C/350°F/Gas 4, for 30 minutes, basting after 15 minutes. Transfer the meat to a warmed dish and keep hot. Strain and measure the stock in which the meat was cooked and make up to 375ml/¾ pint with water.

Heat the butter or margarine in a pan. Stir in the flour and cook gently until browned. Gradually add the stock to the roux and stir until boiling. Reduce the heat and simmer for 5 minutes. Season to taste. Serve the sauce separately.

VITELLO TONNATA

(Cold Veal with Tuna Sauce)

6–8 helpings

5 anchovy fillets
1kg/2lb leg of veal, boned
salt and pepper
pared rind and juice of 1 lemon
1 onion
2 cloves
2 bay leaves

1 medium-sized carrot
2 sticks celery
375ml/¾ pint dry white wine
100g/4oz canned tuna fish in oil
100ml/4fl oz olive oil *or* as needed
1×15ml spoon/1 tablespoon capers

GARNISH
lemon slices

Drain the anchovy fillets. Remove the thin outer skin and any solid fat from the veal. Place 3 anchovy fillets along the length of the cavity where the bone was removed. Reshape the meat and tie it into a neat roll about 20×15cm/8×6 inches. Season the meat. Put it in a stewpan with a strip of lemon rind. Skin the onion, press in the cloves, and add it to the pan with the bay leaves. Slice and add the carrot and celery. Pour in the wine, and add just enough water to cover the meat. Bring to the boil, cover, reduce the heat, and simmer gently for 1½ hours or until the meat is tender. Remove it from the pan and leave to cool completely. (Keep the stock for another dish.)

When the meat is cold, slice it thinly, then reshape it into the roll. Place it in a deep terrine or serving dish.

Pound the tuna fish with its oil, the lemon juice, and remaining anchovy fillets until smooth. Alternatively, process in an electric blender. When smooth, trickle in the olive oil gradually, as when making mayonnaise, whisking or blending as fast as possible until the mixture thickens. Season to taste. Chop and fold in the capers. Pour the sauce over the meat, cover loosely, and leave to marinate for 12–14 hours. Serve garnished with thin lemon slices.

Vitello Tonnata

BRAINS IN BLACK BUTTER

(Cervelles au Beurre Noir)

4 helpings

2 sets calf's brains
salt
1×5ml spoon/1 teaspoon lemon
  juice
1 small onion
1 litre/2 pints water
2×15ml spoons/2 tablespoons
  white wine vinegar

bouquet garni
flour for dusting
ground pepper
2×15ml spoons/2 tablespoons
  butter
butter for greasing

BLACK BUTTER

4×15ml spoons/4 tablespoons
  butter
1×15ml spoon/1 tablespoon white
  wine vinegar

2×15ml spoons/2 tablespoons
  capers (optional)

GARNISH

sprig of parsley

Soak the brains for 30 minutes in lightly salted cold water sharpened with the lemon juice to remove all traces of blood. Meanwhile, skin and halve the onion, and put it in a saucepan with the water, vinegar, and bouquet garni. Heat to simmering point and simmer for 30 minutes. Leave the stock to cool.

Drain the brains, and cut off any membranes. Wash thoroughly but very gently. Put the brains into the stock, heat slowly to simmering point, and poach for 20 minutes. Drain thoroughly, and put into very cold water to cool. Drain again and pat dry. Season the flour with salt and pepper, and dust the brains with it. Heat the 2×15ml spoons/2 tablespoons butter in a frying pan, and fry the brains lightly, turning them over, until just browned on all sides. Put them in a shallow serving dish, and keep them warm under buttered paper.

Take any bits of brains out of the frying pan, add the butter for the Black Butter and heat until golden-brown. Add the vinegar, and let it boil up. As soon as it foams, pour the mixture over the brains, adding the capers, if used. Serve at once, garnished with a sprig of parsley.

HUNGARIAN CALF'S LIVER

6 helpings

625g/1¼lb calf's liver
plain flour
salt
paprika

50g/2oz butter
2×15ml spoons/2 tablespoons
  finely grated onion
100ml/4 fl oz fresh *or* soured cream

Remove the skin and tubes, and cut the liver into 1.25cm/½ inch slices. Season some flour with salt and paprika. Dip the slices of liver in the flour, then shake off the excess. Heat the butter in a frying pan and fry the liver quickly on both sides until browned, then more slowly until tender. Fry the onion with the liver for about 5 minutes. Remove the liver, arrange the slices down the centre of a warmed serving dish, and keep hot. Pour any excess fat out of the pan, add the cream, and heat gently without boiling. Season to taste. Pour this sauce over the liver. Sprinkle with paprika, and serve very hot.

Overleaf
From the left
Ham Slices with Fruit (page 52), *Lamb Shashlik (page 25)* and
Escalopes of Veal (page 40)

PORK, BACON & HAM

MRS BEETON'S ROAST GRISKIN OF PORK

———— *4 helpings* ————

1kg/2lb neck end of chine of pork
 or griskin (see **Note**)
flour for dredging
50g/2oz lard
fat for greasing

1×15ml spoon/1 tablespoon dried
 sage
2×10ml spoons/2 dessertspoons
 flour
250ml/½ pint water
salt and pepper

Wipe the meat and dredge it lightly with flour. Melt the lard in a roasting tin and brush some of it over the meat. Put the meat in the tin and roast it in a hot oven, 220°C/425°F/Gas 7, for 10 minutes. Baste well and cover the meat loosely with greased greaseproof paper. Reduce the heat to moderate, 180°C/350°F/Gas 4, and continue to roast the meat for a further 1¾ hours, basting it often. Ten minutes before the end of the cooking time, take out the meat, sprinkle it with sage, and return to the oven, uncovered, to complete the cooking.

When cooked, transfer the meat to a warmed serving dish and keep hot. Pour off all but 1×15ml spoon/1 tablespoon fat in the roasting tin and retain the sediment. Stir in the flour and cook gently over low heat for 3–4 minutes until the flour is lightly browned. Gradually add the water and stir until the gravy thickens slightly. Taste and season with salt and pepper. Simmer for about 1 minute, then strain the gravy into a warmed sauce-boat.

Serve with apple sauce.

Note The griskin is the backbone, spine or chine of a pig cut away when preparing a side for bacon; or it can be a shoulder of pork stripped of fat. As it is sold without rind or fat, it needs frequent basting.

ROAST, BONED, STUFFED PORK

6 helpings

1.5kg/3lb boned bladebone of pork

3×15ml spoons/3 tablespoons oil

STUFFING

1 medium-sized onion
1 stick of celery
100g/4oz flat mushrooms
25g/1oz butter *or* margarine
50g/2oz canned *or* frozen sweetcorn
50g/2oz white breadcrumbs

1×15ml spoon/1 tablespoon chopped parsley
salt and pepper
1×2.5ml spoon/½ teaspoon ground mace
1×5ml spoon/1 teaspoon lemon juice

Wipe the meat and deeply score the rind of the meat if not done by the butcher.

Make the stuffing. Prepare the onion, celery and mushrooms, and chop them finely. Melt the butter or margarine in a small pan and fry the onion and celery until lightly browned. Remove from the heat. Add the mushrooms, sweetcorn, breadcrumbs and parsley, and mix well. Season to taste, and add the mace and lemon juice.

Spoon the stuffing evenly into the 'pocket' left after the meat was boned. Roll up the joint and tie with thin string at regular intervals. Heat 2×15ml spoons/2 tablespoons oil in a roasting tin, then put in the joint. Brush the rind with the remaining oil and sprinkle generously with salt. Roast in a fairly hot oven, 200°C/400°F/Gas 6, for 20–30 minutes, until the crackling is browned. Reduce the heat to moderate, 180°C/350°F/Gas 4, and continue to cook for 1½ hours or until the internal temperature reaches 85–88°C/185–190°F on a meat thermometer. Transfer the joint to a warmed serving dish, remove the string, and keep the meat hot. Pour off the fat in the roasting tin, then prepare a gravy using the sediment left in the tin.

HAM WITH RAISIN SAUCE

8–10 helpings

1.5–2kg/3–4lb parboiled York
   ham
250g/8oz dark soft brown sugar

cloves
100ml/4fl oz white wine vinegar

RAISIN SAUCE

50g/2oz soft dark brown sugar
1×2.5ml spoon/½ teaspoon
   English mustard
1×15ml spoon/1 tablespoon
   cornflour

75g/3oz seedless raisins
1×15ml spoon/1 tablespoon grated
   orange rind
100ml/4fl oz fresh orange juice
200ml/8fl oz water

Put the ham in a shallow baking tin and bake, uncovered, in a warm oven, 160°C/325°F/Gas 3, for 10 minutes per 500g/1lb meat. Thirty minutes before the end of the cooking time, lift out the meat and remove the rind. Score the fat in a pattern of diamonds. Cover the fat with brown sugar and press in cloves at the points of the diamond pattern. Trickle the wine vinegar gently over the ham. Continue baking, basting with the juices, until the ham is fully cooked.

Make the Raisin Sauce. Mix together in a saucepan the brown sugar, mustard and cornflour. Add the rest of the ingredients and cook very gently for 10 minutes or until syrupy.

Transfer the cooked ham to a warmed serving dish and serve the sauce separately in a sauce-boat.

Ham with Raisin Sauce

HAM SLICES WITH FRUIT

3 main-course or 6 light first-course or supper helpings

6 ham *or* gammon slices *or* steaks
  (1.25cm/½ inch thick approx)
150g/5oz soft light brown sugar

75g/3oz soft white breadcrumbs
200ml/8floz pineapple juice

GARNISH

2 apples

75g/3oz margarine

Remove the rind from the ham or gammon and snip the fat at intervals to prevent curling. Put the slices or steaks in a frying pan with a very little water, heat to simmering point, and simmer for 10 minutes, turning them once. Drain. Lay the slices or steaks in an overlapping layer in a large, shallow, ovenproof baking dish. Mix together the sugar and breadcrumbs, and spread it over the slices or steaks, then trickle the pineapple juice over them. Bake uncovered, in a moderate oven, 180°C/350°F/Gas 4, for 25 minutes.

Meanwhile, peel, core, and cut the apples into rings, 2.5cm/1 inch thick (approx). Melt the margarine in a frying pan, and fry the rings until tender but not soft. Decorate the cooked dish with the apple rings, and serve at once.

PORK SAUSAGES WITH CABBAGE

4 helpings

1 hard white cabbage
  (1kg/2lb approx)
1 small onion
75g/3oz butter

salt and pepper
125ml/¼ pint water
500g/1lb pork sausages
  (50g/2oz each)

Trim the cabbage, and cut it into quarters. Shred it finely lengthways. Skin and chop the onion finely. Melt the butter in a large saucepan, and fry the onion in it until transparent. Add the cabbage, salt and pepper, and water. Cover the pan with a tight-fitting lid and cook over gentle heat for 1 hour.

Meanwhile, fry, bake or grill the sausages until cooked through. Drain any liquid from the cooked cabbage and pile the vegetable on a warmed serving dish. Arrange the hot sausages on or around the cabbage.

FRIED SAUSAGES.

GAMMON STEAKS WITH MARMALADE

4 helpings

4 medium-sized gammon steaks
ground pepper
1 small onion
1 × 5ml spoon/1 teaspoon butter *or*
  margarine

4 × 15ml spoons/4 tablespoons
  medium-cut orange marmalade
2 × 5ml spoons/2 teaspoons vinegar

GARNISH

chopped parsley

Remove the rind from the gammon steaks and snip the fat at intervals to prevent curling. Place on a grill rack and season with pepper to taste. Cook under a moderate grill, turning once, for 10–15 minutes depending on the thickness of the steaks. When cooked, transfer the steaks to a warmed serving dish and keep hot.

Skin the onion and chop it finely. Melt the fat in a pan and cook the onion gently for 5 minutes without browning it. Draw the pan off the heat and stir in the marmalade and vinegar, with any fat and juices left in the grill pan. Return to the heat and heat to boiling point, to reduce slightly.

Spoon the sauce over the gammon steaks. Garnish with chopped parsley and serve at once.

GRILLED CRUMBED PORK CHOPS OR CUTLETS

6 helpings

6 pork chops *or* cutlets
1 egg
1×5ml spoon/1 teaspoon dried
  sage

salt and pepper
soft white breadcrumbs
3×15ml spoons/3 tablespoons oil

Wipe the chops or cutlets and trim off any excess fat. Beat the egg until liquid and mix with the sage, salt and pepper. Brush the chops or cutlets on both sides with the beaten egg, then coat them carefully with the breadcrumbs. Brush carefully with some oil, then brush the grill rack with the remaining oil. Cook under a moderate grill for about 20 minutes, turning often, until golden-brown and cooked through.

MRS BEETON'S OXFORD SAUSAGES

Makes 36 sausages or 60–70 chipolatas

1.5kg/3lb pork *or* 0.5kg/1lb lean
   pork, 0.5kg/1lb lean veal and
   0.5kg/1lb beef dripping
500g/1lb soft white breadcrumbs
1×5ml spoon/1 teaspoon ground
   pepper

grated rind of ½ lemon
grated nutmeg
6 chopped sage leaves
1×2.5ml spoon/½ teaspoon
   chopped winter savory
1×2.5ml spoon/½ teaspoon
   marjoram

Choose pork which consists of two-thirds lean meat to one third
fat, without skin and gristle. Cut it up roughly and mince it finely
or coarsely, according to taste; for a fine cut, however, it must be
put through the coarse plate first, otherwise it will clog the
machine. Mix the rest of the ingredients into the sausage-meat and
mince again. Fill the sausage-meat into skins using a
sausage-filler, or make it into little cakes or cork shapes. Allow to
mature for 12–14 hours in a cool place, to develop flavour and
texture.

THE NUTMEG.

BRAISED PORK CHOPS IN CIDER

4 helpings

4 middle loin *or* fore loin pork
 chops
4 × 15ml spoons/4 tablespoons dry
 cider
bouquet garni
2 medium-sized onions
2 cooking apples
a pinch of ground cinnamon

salt and pepper
100g/4oz flat mushrooms
200g/7oz shelled fresh peas
200g/7oz canned whole small
 beetroots
150–200g/5–7oz noodles

Wipe the chops and trim off the rind and excess fat. Heat the rind
and fat trimmings in a frying pan until the fat runs. Add the chops
and fry, turning once, until golden-brown on both sides. Remove
the chops and place them in a casserole. Pour off the excess fat in
the frying pan and reserve the rest. Pour the cider over the chops
and add the bouquet garni. Cover the casserole and cook over
gentle heat or in a warm oven, 160°C/325°F/Gas 3.

Meanwhile, prepare and chop the onions and apples. Put them
into the frying pan and fry gently for 5 minutes. Add the cinnamon
and just enough water to cover the onions and apples. Cover the
pan, heat to simmering point, and simmer for about 15 minutes,
until soft. Rub through a sieve, season to taste, and spoon the
apple and onion mixture over the chops in the casserole. Replace
the lid and cook for 1¾–2 hours in all.

Clean the mushrooms and slice thickly; add them and the peas
for the last 30 minutes of the cooking time. Heat the beetroot
separately. Cook the noodles in boiling salted water until, when
tested, the centre is still slightly firm. Drain the noodles and
beetroot. Serve the noodles on a warmed serving dish with the
chops on top, and arrange the mushrooms, peas, and beetroots
round them.

Braised Pork Chops in Cider

PORK AND APPLE HOT POT

4 helpings

4 loin *or* spare rib chops
1 medium-sized cooking apple
1 medium-sized onion
50g/2oz lard *or* oil
100g/4oz mushrooms

fat for greasing
1×2.5ml spoon/½ teaspoon dried
   sage *or* savory
500g/1lb potatoes
salt and pepper

GARNISH

chopped parsley

Wipe the chops and trim off any excess fat. Prepare the apple and onion and slice them thinly. Heat the lard or oil in a pan and fry the apple and onion until golden-brown. Clean and slice the mushrooms.

Grease a casserole and put the mushrooms in the bottom. Lay the chops on the mushrooms and cover with the apple and onion. Sprinkle the herb over the top. Prepare the potatoes and cut them into 1.25cm/½ inch cubes. Top the casserole with the potatoes and brush them with the fat remaining in the pan. Season with salt and pepper. Pour in enough water to come half-way up the meat and vegetables. Cover the pan with a tight-fitting lid and cook in a moderate oven, 180°C/350°F/Gas 4, for 1½ hours. Remove the lid 30 minutes before the end of the cooking time to allow the potatoes to brown. Garnish with chopped parsley and serve from the casserole.

FAGGOTS OR SAVOURY DUCKS

800g/1lb 10oz pig's liver
100g/4oz fat belly of pork
2 medium-sized onions
a pinch of dried thyme
1×2.5ml spoon/½ teaspoon dried
   sage
a pinch of dried basil (optional)

salt and pepper
a pinch of grated nutmeg
1 egg
100g/4oz soft white breadcrumbs
caul fat *or* flour, as preferred
fat for greasing

Remove the skin and tubes of the liver, then slice it. Slice the pork belly. Skin and slice the onions. Put the meat and onions in a saucepan with just enough water to cover them. Heat to boiling point, cover the pan, reduce the heat, and simmer for 30 minutes. Strain off the liquid and reserve it for the gravy.

Mince the meat and onions finely. Add the herbs, salt, pepper, and nutmeg. Beat the egg until liquid and stir it in. Mix in enough breadcrumbs to make a mixture which can be moulded. Divide it into 8 equal portions and shape them into round balls. Cut squares of caul fat, if used, large enough to encase the balls and wrap each ball in a piece of fat. Alternatively, roll each ball in flour. Lay the faggots side by side in a greased baking tin. Cover the tin loosely with foil. Bake in a moderate oven, 180°C/350°F/Gas 4, for 25 minutes. Remove the foil and bake for 10 minutes to brown the tops of the faggots.

Serve hot, with a thickened gravy made from the cooking liquid.

PIG'S TROTTERS IN JELLY

4 pig's trotters
2 pig's ears
1 × 10ml spoon/1 dessertspoon
  chopped parsley

1 × 2.5ml spoon/½ teaspoon
  chopped fresh sage
salt and pepper

Singe off the hairs. Wash the trotters and ears thoroughly in salted water. Scald the ears. Put the trotters and ears in a large pan with just enough cold water to cover them. Heat to boiling point, cover the pan with a tight-fitting lid, reduce the heat, and simmer gently for about 3 hours until the bones can be removed easily. Lift out the trotters and ears, reserving the liquid in the pan. Cut the meat into neat dice and replace in the liquid. Add the herbs, and season to taste. Simmer gently for 15 minutes. Turn into a mould or basin and leave until cold and set.

SAGE.

Acknowledgements

Photography by Grant Symon

Home Economist   Linda Fraser

Stylist   Shirley Melville

The publisher would like to thank David Mellor for kindly loaning equipment for photography.